Critical Thinking
Essentials

Quick Reference Handbook

Captain Kevin M. Smith

Author of the **Commitment to Reason Series**

Cover design by Jennifer Guter, Reflections Printing
Interior design by Mary Jean Archival

Published in the United States of America

ISBN: 978-0-69209-655-0

BUSINESS & ECONOMICS / Decision-Making & Problem Solving

18.11.27

Critical Thinking

An Idea Whose Time Has Come

Web Site: www.commitmenttoreason.com

Handbook

This quick reference handbook is a companion to the Commitment to Reason series.

Commitment to Reason Series

Family of Products:

**Books-eBooks-Audio
Books-Handbooks-Tutorials
Podcasts-Newsletters-Lecture Series**

Welcome
to the World of
Critical Thinking

Prepare to be amazed!

Clarify-Reason-Win

**Clarify the actual. Employ reason.
Gain winning performance.**

Dedication

This handbook on critical thinking is dedicated
to the memory of

Colonel John Boyd, USAF
(1927–1997)

America's greatest strategic thinker
of modern times

Creator of the OODA Loop
and the Power Equation

Contents

Foreword

Today's individual has access to technology and resources that the most powerful national governments would have been envious of only decades ago. Endless knowledge is available at our fingertips through the Internet. We can create and collaborate with anyone anywhere in the world without ever having met them in person. Yet despite the wonders we have available to us, some of history's most pressing issues remain. Economic turmoil, disease, and conflict continue to loom. How can we apply the tools we have in order to meet these challenges?

We start by drilling down, by understanding ourselves and our biases to the issues, by working out what the problem truly is so that we can meet it with the appropriate response. *We think critically!*

Challenging environments have a way of encouraging critical thinking. Those who are unable to effectively identify and address the root cause of an issue in an environment of limited time and resources will quickly be swept aside. Few understand this better than combat aviators, of which Captain Kevin Smith is one. While serving in the US Navy, Captain Smith saw tours of duty as a carrier-based fighter pilot, Top Gun instructor, operations officer, and squadron commander. He was later involved in the design of the crew station for the F-22 Raptor, one of the most advanced combat aircraft in the world today. Captain Smith also accumulated over 25,000 hours of flying time in various Boeing jetliners while a United Airlines captain. The FAA, having recognized Captain Smith's ability to identify problems and develop solutions, put him on the original team charged with redesigning airline pilot training for all US carriers.

The *Critical Thinking Essentials Quick Reference Handbook* is Captain Smith's formula, gained through years of experience and research, for successful critical thinking. It is simple enough to be accessible, but has enough depth to continue providing insight as your understanding grows. Take this guide and exercise your ability to think critically. Challenge the problems that affect you personally and move on to the larger issues from there. Humanity needs people who are willing to peek behind the curtain and confront the wizard.

Ryan Hinkley
Portsmouth, NH

Part I
Preparing the Reader

Fundamental Argument for Critical Thinking

*In life what is most important is not **what** you think but **how** you think.*

Critical *thinking is key.*

Before you consider an issue, stop and ask yourself, how *should* I think about this?

Life's Most Important Decision

Employ Critical Thinking

Either **embrace reason**
or
do that which is **hostile to reason.**

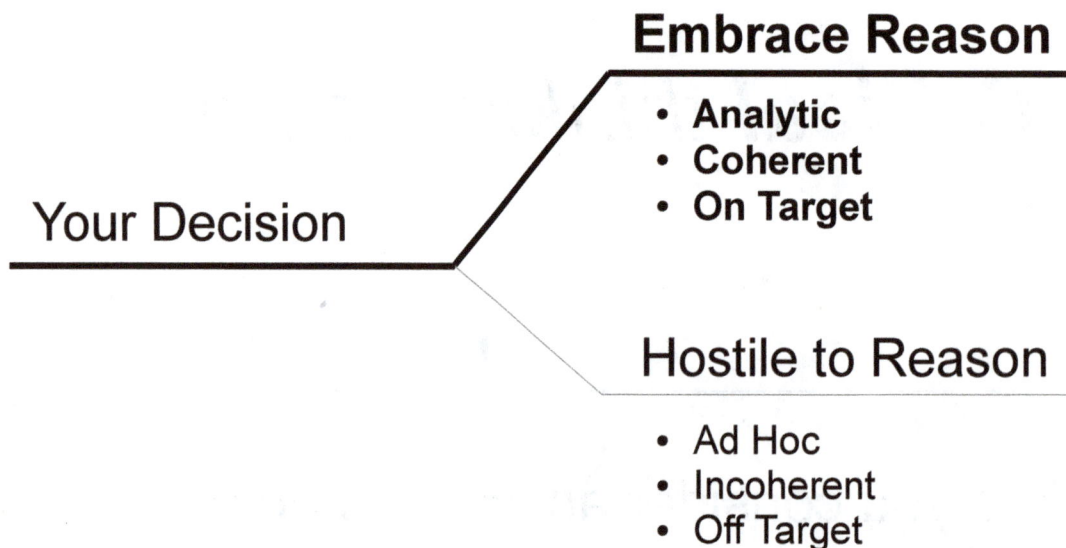

Embrace Reason

- **Analytic**
- **Coherent**
- **On Target**

Your Decision

Hostile to Reason

- Ad Hoc
- Incoherent
- Off Target

Figure 1. Employ Critical Thinking

Critical Thinking Concepts

Preparing to Build the Critical Thinking Model

How information processing occurs in a critical thinking algorithm:

1. Information is received about some aspect of reality: the state of the world, your environment, business, operation, or mission.

2. This information is determined to be either important or not important.

3. Further considerations are made concerning level of significance and urgency generated by this revealed information.

4. The problem, challenge, or issue is then clearly specified. This is done without any reference to a possible solution.

5. A range of solution options (alternatives) are specified that may prove effective in dealing with the problem, challenge, or issue.

6. The best option (alternative) is selected based upon defined selection criteria.

7. The option is executed to achieve success.

8. Ongoing performance is measured and corrections are made if necessary.

A Useful Definition of Critical Thinking

Critical thinking is used to correct the most common and persistent problems associated with errors of judgment and choice. Evidence has shown that these errors are often committed by amateurs and experts alike.

Importantly, critical thinking is a defined conceptual construct and set of cognitive performance aids of proven value that when activated sharpens observations, clarifies the actual, improves problem solving, and optimizes success.

Critical thinking is a skill that can be learned, lends itself to practice, and when used with intent, can achieve amazing results.

A growing body of evidence profoundly suggests that critical thinking is needed now more than ever due to our diminishing ability as individuals and as a nation to solve problems effectively and efficiently.

Part II

Presenting
the Critical Thinking Model

Critical Thinking Model

Observe with clarity. Observe the world and your immediate surroundings objectively. Reality is an objective fact. Extreme care must be taken to avoid observing with the goal of supporting one's most cherished belief. One must be consistent in *clarifying the actual*.

Employ reason. The critical thinker uses the power of reason to determine a specific course of action necessary to achieve success. "Employing reason" also means to be analytical: use an analytic process to address all significant challenges. Avoid that which is ad hoc. *Employ analytic reasoning.*

Perform well. Do what is necessary and do it well. Always do your best. This involves taking action, and directing others if needed, to achieve winning performance. The goal is always mission success, not personal glory. *Perform with precision.*

Clarify the actual.	Employ analytic reasoning.	Perform with precision.

Table 1. Critical Thinking Model

Depiction of the
Critical Thinking Model

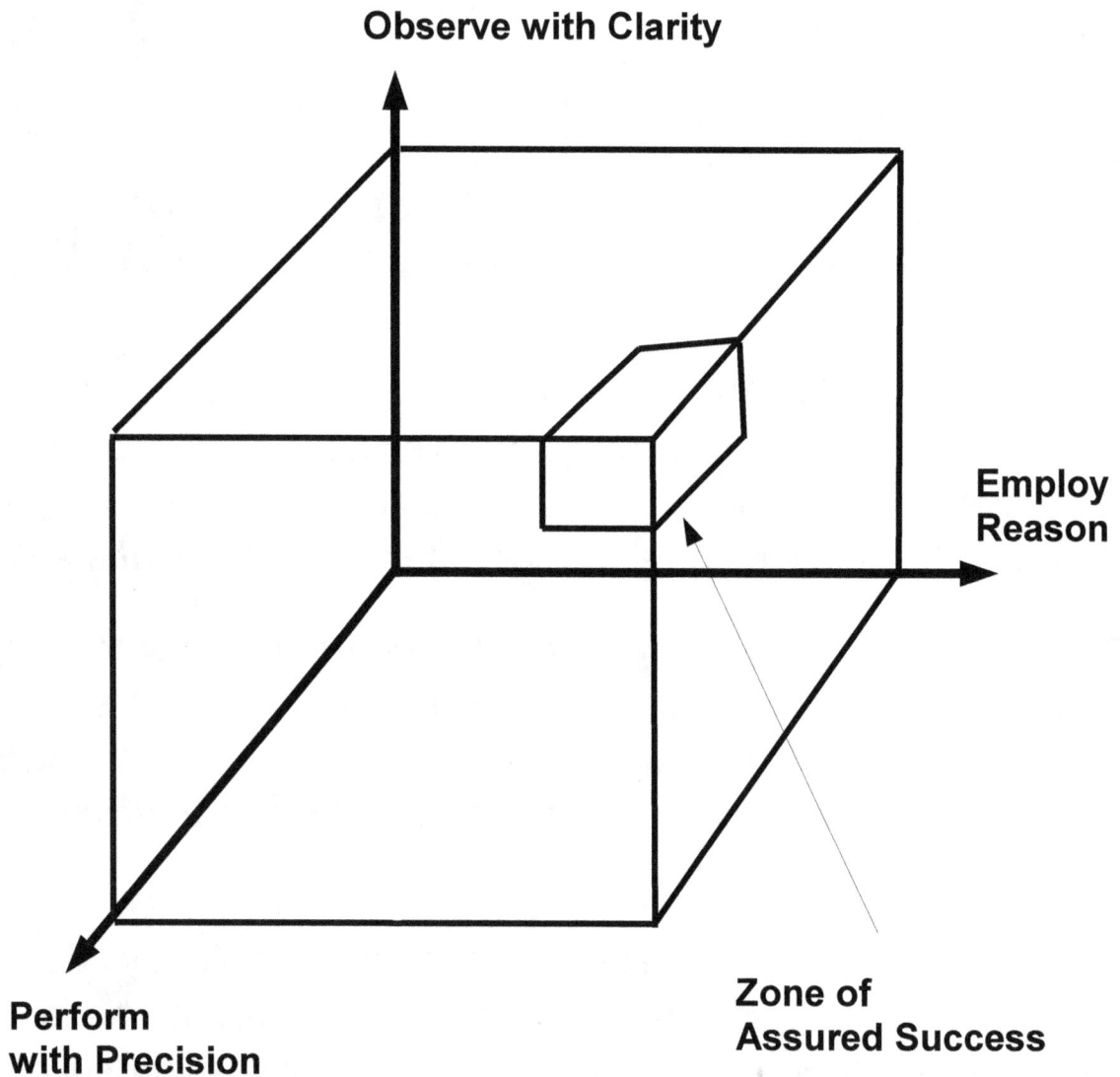

Observe with Clarity

Employ Reason

Perform with Precision

Zone of Assured Success

Depiction of the three main components of critical thinking and the area where success can be assured. Outside of this area success is less likely.

Figure 2. Depiction of the Critical Thinking Model

Critical Thinking Model
Expanded Version

Critical Thinking Essential	Element	Discussion
Observe	Situate	Situate yourself to enhance data reception.
	Detect	Detect signals that may be significant.
	Orient	Orient events to optimize clarity.
Reason	Analyze	Analyze and generate alternatives.
	Evaluate	Evaluate each alternative for utility.
	Decide	Decide on best alternative to achieve mission success.
Perform	Execute	Execute chosen alternative.
	Measure	Measure ongoing performance.
	Optimize	Apply necessary course corrections.

Table 2. Critical Thinking Model, Expanded Version

Flowchart

The following section is a type of flowchart to help provide additional explanation of the front-to-back critical thinking process. This explanation uses a yes-or-no format to illustrate certain decision aspects related to critical thinking, as well as some iterations that may be necessary. Flowcharts are most useful in the design process. For readers that are involved in the design of training programs that address critical thinking, this flowchart will be especially helpful. The yes-or-no process takes the form shown below in figure 3.

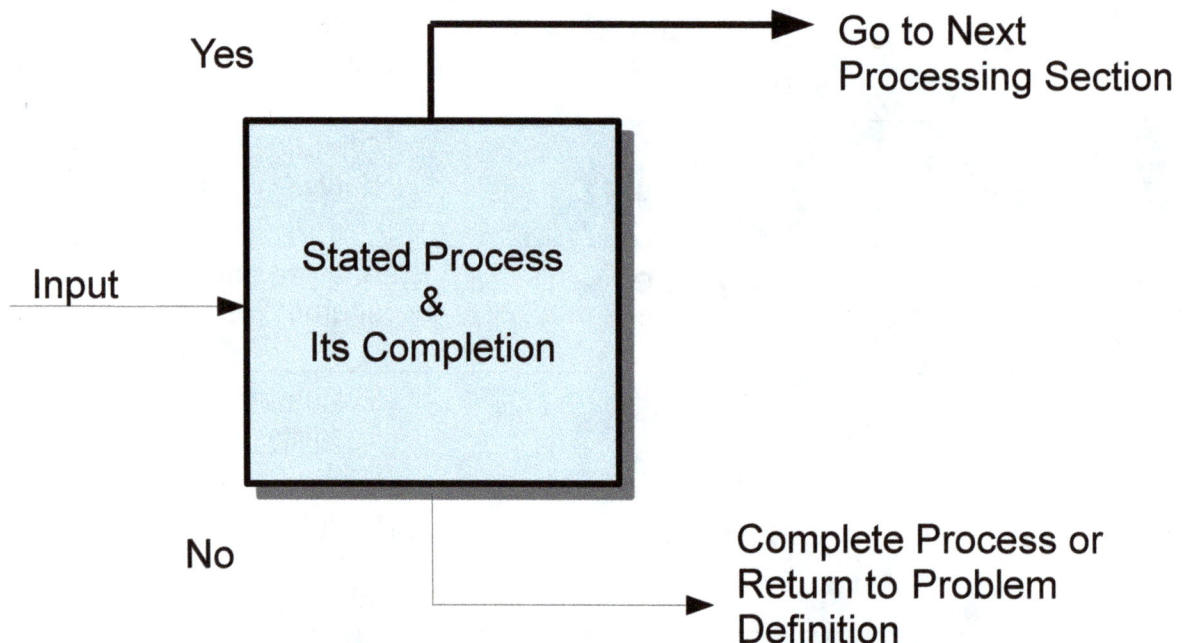

Figure 3. Yes/No Flowchart

Two versions of the critical thinking flowchart are presented. The first version, figure 4 shown on the next page, is the simplified version. This is followed by the second version, a more detailed treatment for those readers that wish a greater level of specifics.

Critical Thinking Flowchart
Simplified Version

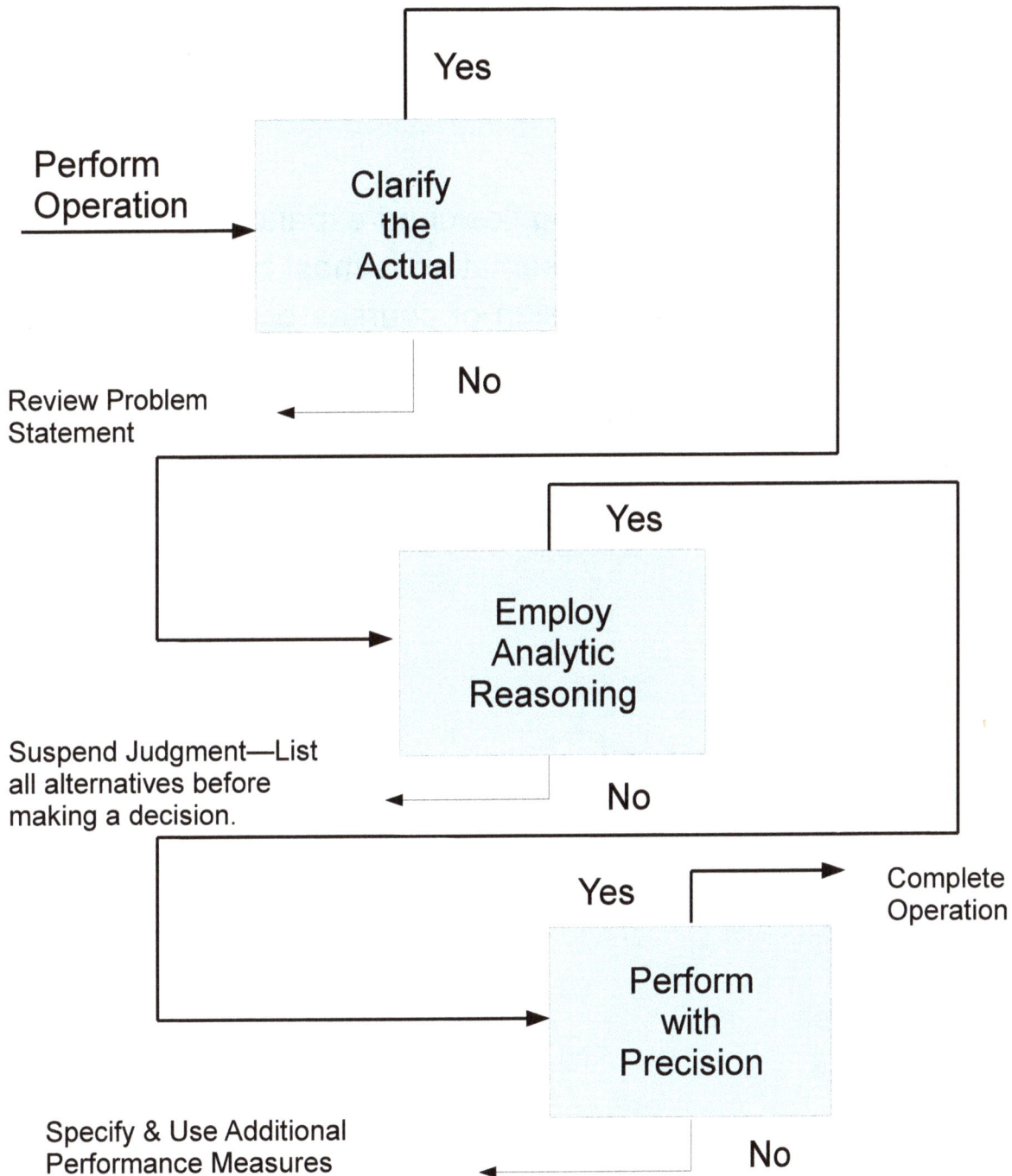

Yes

Perform
Operation

Clarify
the
Actual

No

Review Problem
Statement

Yes

Employ
Analytic
Reasoning

No

Suspend Judgment—List
all alternatives before
making a decision.

Yes

Complete
Operation

Perform
with
Precision

No

Specify & Use Additional
Performance Measures

Figure 4. Critical Thinking Flowchart, Simplified Version

Critical Thinking Flowchart
Expanded Version

What follows is the critical thinking flowchart expanded version shown in figures 5, 6, and 7. This representation is most beneficial for those professionals involved in the design of courses or training programs that address various aspects of critical thinking. This flowchart can also serve as a syllabus outline for specialized courses that target critical thinking.

Observe

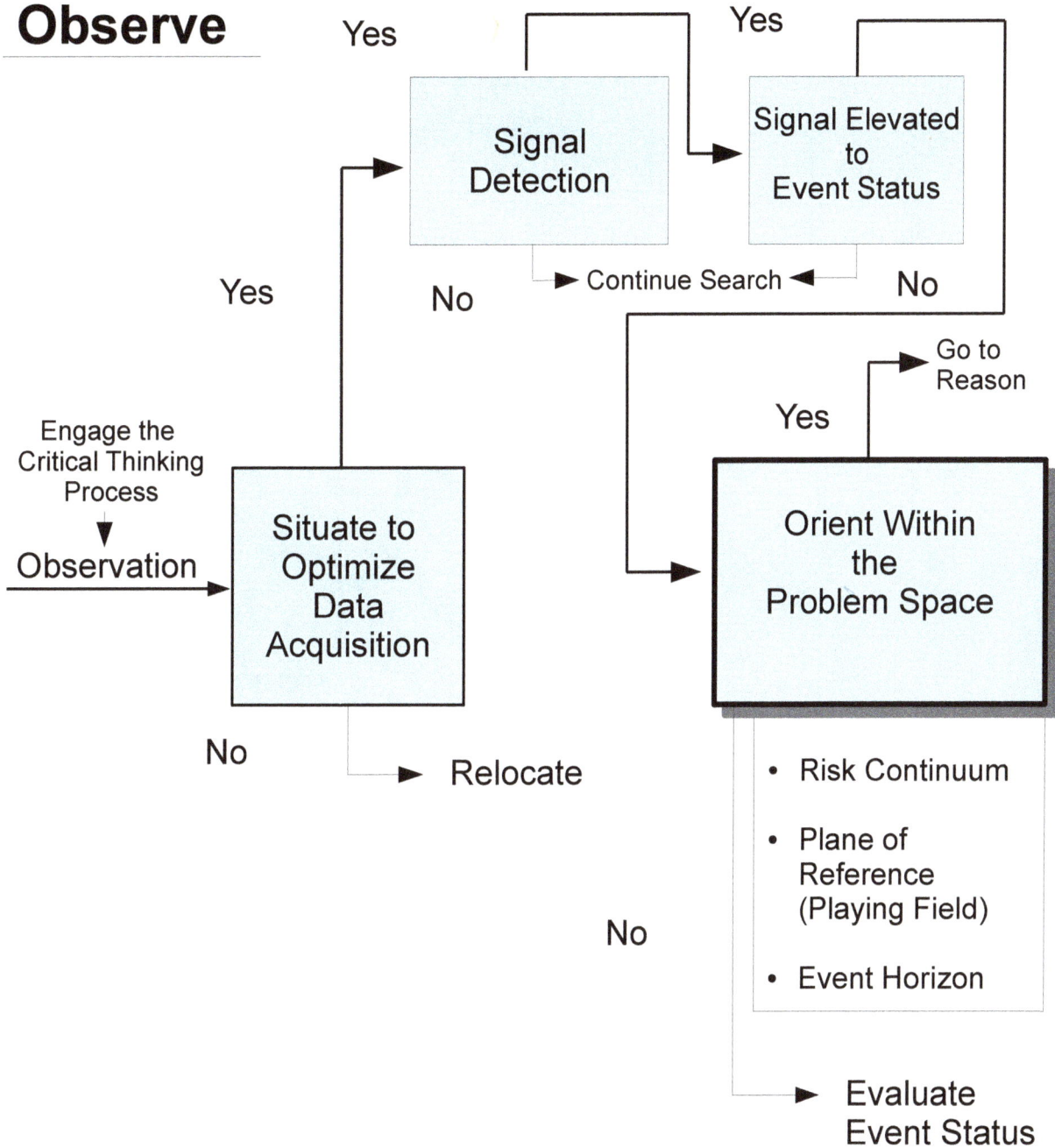

Yes

Yes

Signal Detection

Signal Elevated to Event Status

Yes

No → Continue Search ← No

Go to Reason

Yes

Engage the Critical Thinking Process

Observation

Situate to Optimize Data Acquisition

Orient Within the Problem Space

No

Relocate

- Risk Continuum

- Plane of Reference (Playing Field)

- Event Horizon

No

Evaluate Event Status

Objective: Observe with clarity such that you are able to recognize the actual.

Figure 5. Observe

Reason

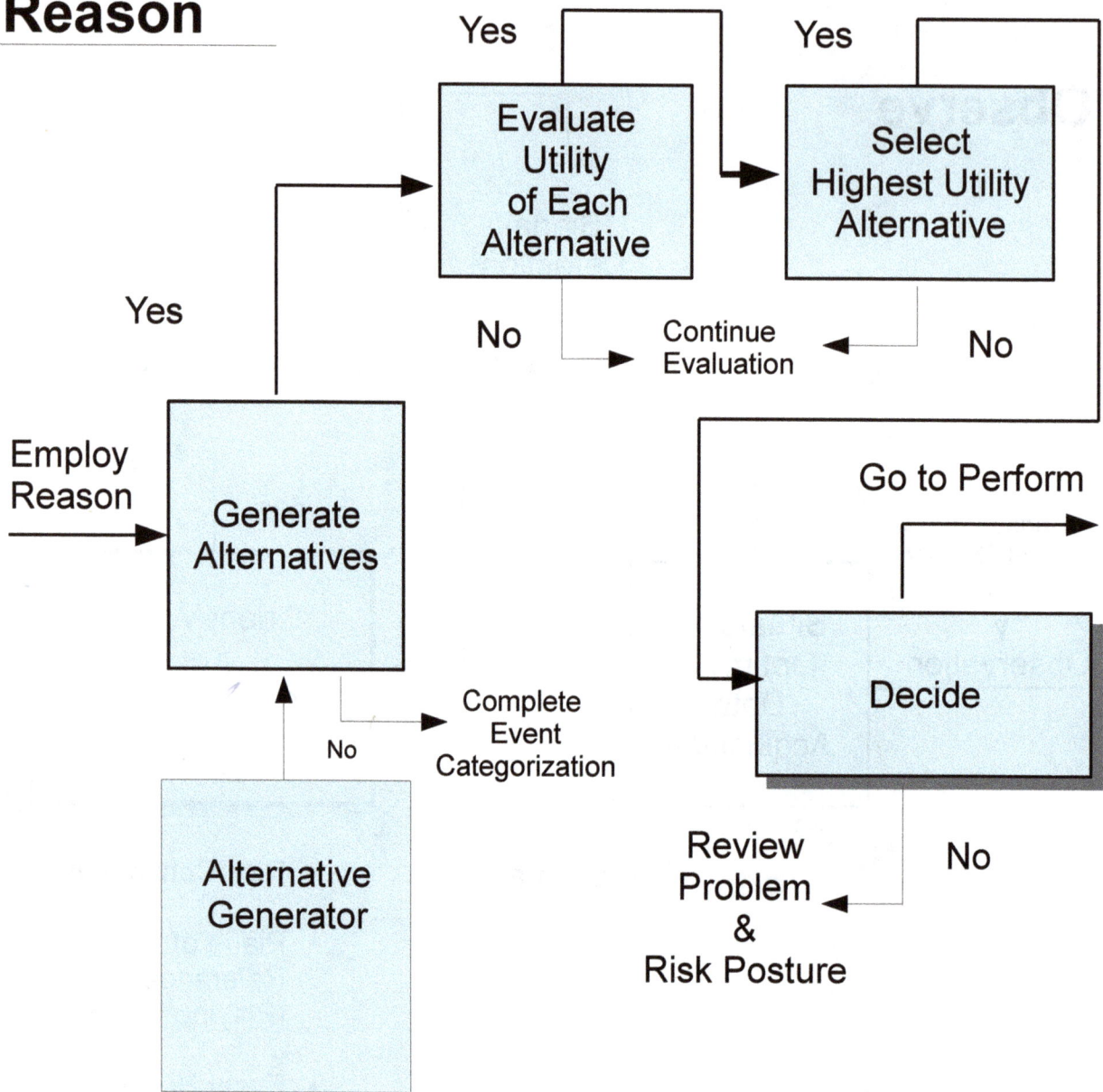

Objective: Employ analytic reasoning to uncover the ingredients for success. Mission success is the central focus.

Figure 6. Reason

Perform

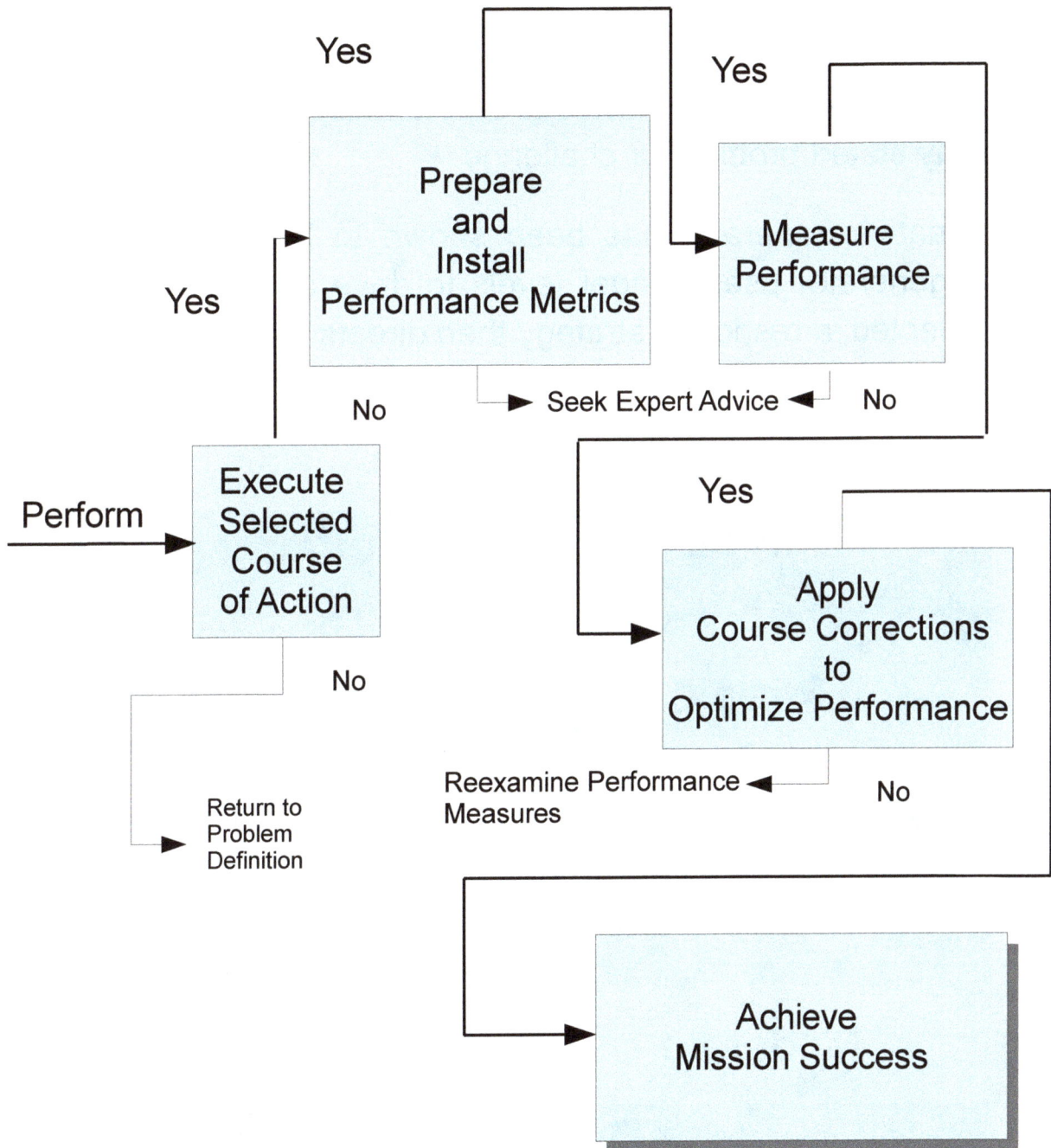

Yes   Yes

Prepare and Install Performance Metrics

Measure Performance

Yes

No   Seek Expert Advice   No

Perform   **Execute Selected Course of Action**

Yes

Apply Course Corrections to Optimize Performance

No

Return to Problem Definition

Reexamine Performance Measures   No

Achieve Mission Success

Objective: Perform in a way that will help ensure mission success. One should always strive for excellence.

Figure 7. Perform

Alternative Generator

The challenge for the critical thinker is how one can generate alternatives in the first place in order to arrive at a potentially viable solution to the previously stated problem or challenge.

An alternative generator has been shown to be especially useful. Such a generator uses danger levels to drive a response category. Once selected, a response strategy then directs the formulation of the response activity package.

Table 3 below will help illustrate this concept.

Danger Zone	Response Category
Extreme	Escape
Very High	Terminate
High	Abandon
Moderate	Modify
Low	Continue

Table 3. Alternative Generator

Many programs and operations could have been kept from becoming a catastrophe if danger levels were known and used.

Part III

More Details
on the
Critical Thinking Model

Observe

Situate. Situate yourself to optimize signal detection (incoming information). Activate all available sensors. Establish a mind-set and frame of reference that will aid in signal detection.

Detect. Detect all incoming signals. Do not ignore that which may run counter to a closely held belief or belief system. Discriminate between significant and insignificant signals. Consider whether or not the detected signal rises to event status.

Orient. Orient the detected signal (incoming information) to improve clarity. In this step, "clarify the actual" is a critical activity. Many initiatives fail because they deal with the wrong issue or problem.

Orient the detected signal with respect to the *problem space*. The problem space is a conceptual structure consisting of the following:

- Event status: The detected signal has been characterized as an event. This is accomplished by orienting (locating) the detected signal on the risk continuum.
- Playing field: Orient the event with respect to the operating environment in which it exists. Do not attempt to play football on a baseball field, or vice versa.
- Event horizon: Orient the event with respect to the event horizon. The event horizon contains all events and mission critical elements that are likely to have a significant impact on the plan, operation, or mission.
- Problem definition: Create the formal problem statement. Keep the statement pure; that is, without any reference to a possible solution. The problem statement should be comprehensive and analytic.
- Challenge statement: The challenge statement is derived from the problem statement and covers such things as availability of resources and other constraints.

Reason

Analyze. Reason is the major problem solving step, with analytics as its major component. This analytic process involves conceptualizing and listing all plausible alternatives that could likely bring solutions to bear on the previously stated problem. Be creative. Do not limit oneself because of lack of self-confidence or politics or what others may think. Experience, expert advice, and especially innovation are important. For mission critical events, it is helpful to use the danger zone template to help generate appropriate alternatives.

Evaluate. Subject each alternative to an evaluation that includes the ability of each to perform that which is necessary to achieve success. Often this is determined using utility analysis. The utility of an object or concept is calculated by considering its intrinsic value and the probability or likelihood that it will be available.

Decide. This is the actual decision-making step. First, organize all plausible alternatives in descending order based on the calculated utility. Then look at the list to see if any gaps, or omissions, are evident. Add to the list if needed. Finally, select the alternative with the highest utility. Maximum utility is the key.

$$\text{Utility} = \text{Value} \times \text{Probability}$$

Perform

Execute. Execute the initiative that represents the selected alternative. Often this involves performing an activity package that may be available or may need to be created. Typically, you can locate a preferred strategy so that the activity package will not need to be created from scratch.

Measure. Prepare and install performance metrics to help evaluate performance. Measure ongoing performance at key measurement points. Graphs, trajectories, trend lines, and standard deviations may be useful.

Optimize. Apply course corrections in order to optimize performance and achieve mission success. Anticipate early and apply small corrections. It is often helpful to look at actual, ongoing performance at a higher level of abstraction, that is, strategically.

This entails factoring in the level of risk that has been encountered.

Playing Field
Additional Discussion on the Frame of Reference

Risk Posture

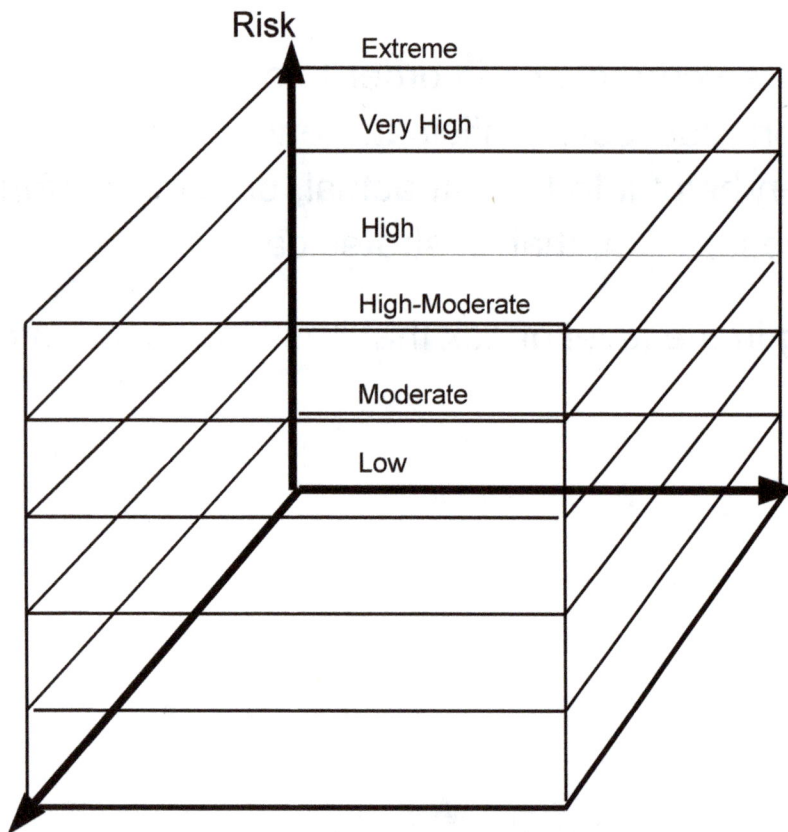

Note: Select the optimum playing field based upon the current or expected risk posture for all recognizable problems. Do not downplay or ignore risk. Also, do not operate on a playing field that does not correspond to the actual risk encountered.

Caution: Do not apply the *right* solution to the *wrong* problem.

Figure 8. Risk Posture

Playing Field Discussion

The fact that a particular problem or challenge needs to go through an orientation phase first before entering the solution phase is an important aspect of applied critical thinking. Conceptualizing the problem with respect to the appropriate playing field is an important step on the way to formulating an optimum solution. Different playing fields are used for different types of problems. These can be organized around levels of risk or particular danger zone categories.

These danger zones are (1) extreme, (2) very high, (3) high, (4) high-moderate, (5) moderate, and (6) low.

Experience has shown that in a large number of cases—such as a business failure, major accident, defeat on the battlefield, or failed government program—the failure can be traced to its root cause: an attempt to apply the *right* solution to the *wrong* problem. By "right" solution we mean the solution most favored by many including most of the so-called experts. By "wrong" problem, we mean that a clear understanding of the problem was lacking because, in part, the appropriate playing field was not used. Instead, a default playing field that tended to support the favored solution was used. This of course almost always leads to failure.

Caution: Do not attempt to formulate a solution to a problem while operating from the wrong playing field (plane of reference). This will inevitably lead to failure. The risk associated with a recognizable operational problem is often understated, thus resulting in the formulation of a moderate-risk solution in response to increasingly dangerous, high-risk situation. This is the greatest single cause of most performance failures, and is a lesson learned time and again when studying airline accidents.

Playing Field Discussion
(Continued)

Danger Level	Description
Extreme	Catastrophe imminent
Very High	Operational parameters exceeded
High	Total risk excessive
High-Moderate	Moderate risk becoming increasingly problematic
Moderate	Moderate risk of concern
Low	Continue normal operations

Mission Critical Event →

Figure 9. Danger Field and Discussion for Mission Critical Events

The encountered mission critical event must be related to a particular danger zone and category. This is necessary to clarify the actual danger that is impacting the operation or mission.

Playing Field Discussion (Continued)

Caution: Do not attempt a solution operating from the wrong playing field.

Assumption: A plan is being executed, an operation is being performed, or a mission is being conducted.

Low-risk playing field: Risk is low, operation is routine, and so continue with current plan.

Moderate-risk playing field: Operational risk has risen to moderate; therefore, modify the operation to accommodate the moderate risk profile.

Danger: High-risk playing field. Abandon the current operation. Some delay is acceptable to formulate an alternative plan.

Danger: Very high-risk playing field. Terminate the operation without undue delay. Conditions no longer safe.

Danger: Extreme risk playing field. Execute escape without delay. Conditions extreme.

What-How Orientation
Critical Examination of a Particular Issue

The conceptual construct presented in this section involves the critical examination of a particular issue to measure its importance. The concept is straightforward. The higher the level of expressed certitude concerning what has been asserted, correspondingly, the higher the level of analytic inquiry (critical examination) required in order to confirm the validity of the argument. The graph shown below (figure 10) can be helpful. This is called the what-how graph. Here the X axis represents the level of certitude of *what* has been asserted. The corresponding Y axis represents *how* this assertion has come to be known, and the level to which a critical examination of the assertion is required in order to confirm its validity.

What-How Graph

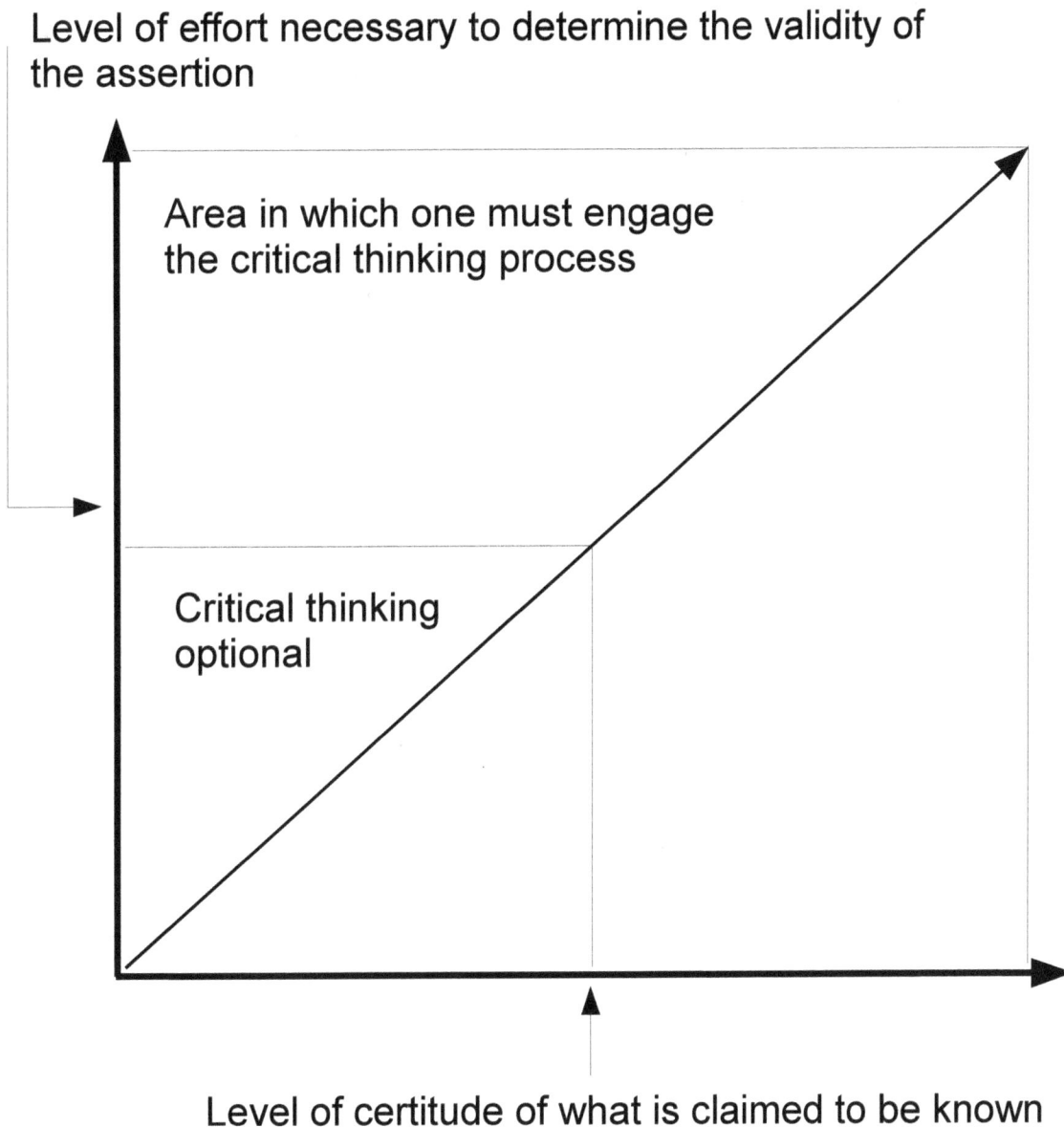

Level of effort necessary to determine the validity of the assertion

Area in which one must engage the critical thinking process

Critical thinking optional

Level of certitude of what is claimed to be known

Figure 10. What-How Graph

- What is it that we know, and how certain are we?
- How do we know what we know?
- How do we know what we don't know?

The Operational Decision Algorithm

On the next page we have represented the operational decision algorithm in figure 11. This decision algorithm directly relates to the previous playing field discussion, and is presented for those who desire more information of a decision-processing nature. Knowledge of how operational decisions are performed is most useful for those conducting complex, high-risk endeavors such as air and space operations, surface ship and submarine operations, various military operations, mountain climbing, and so forth.

Notice that the risk posture is the same as previously addressed in the playing field discussion. Thus, for each level of danger, there is a corresponding frame of reference (playing field) as well as a corresponding decision analytic structure. These two aspects of critical thinking form an essential interaction that supports optimum decision processing, ensuring success.

Operational Decision Making

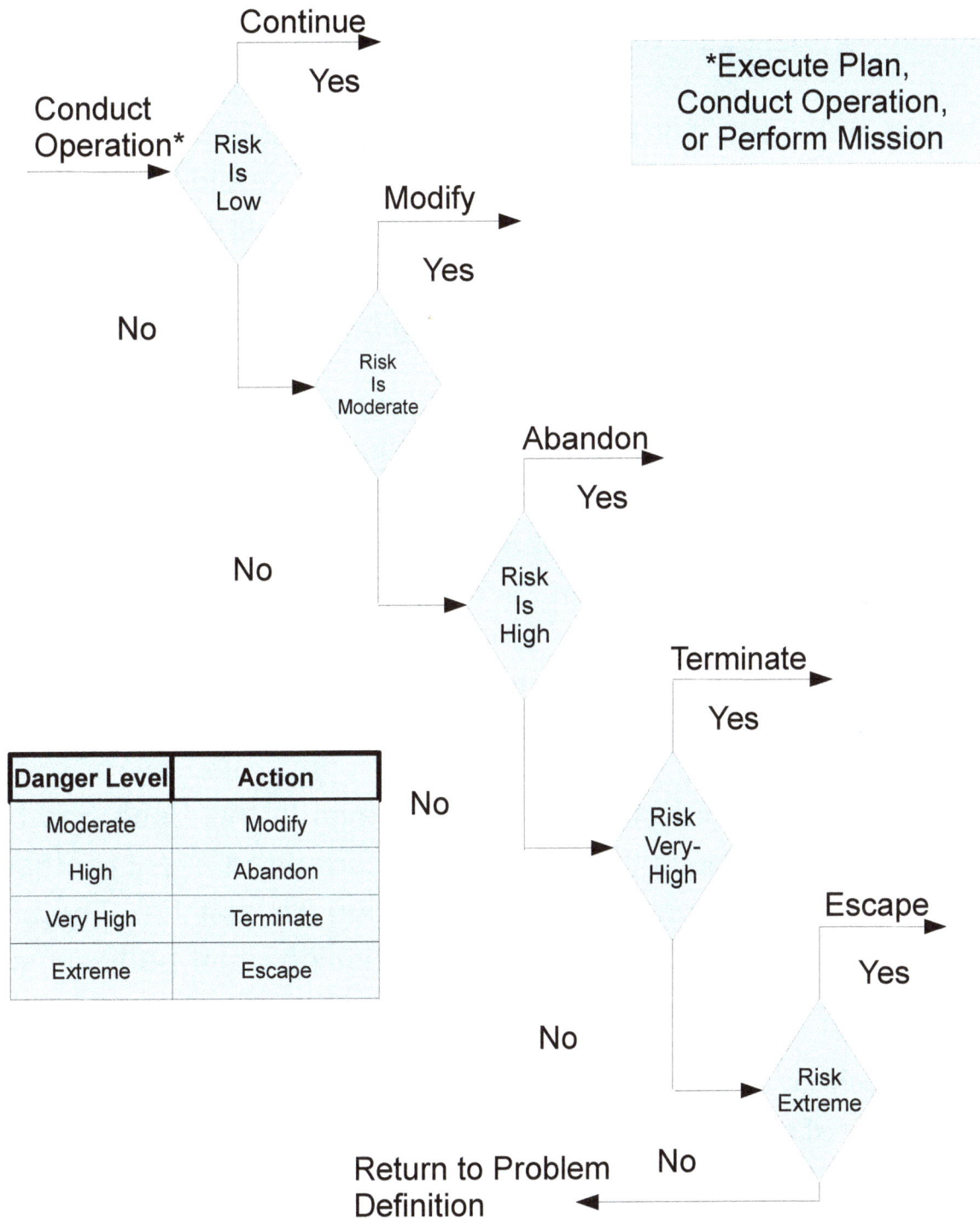

Continue

Yes

Conduct
Operation*

*Execute Plan,
Conduct Operation,
or Perform Mission

Risk
Is
Low

Modify

Yes

No

Risk
Is
Moderate

Abandon

Yes

No

Risk
Is
High

Terminate

Yes

No

Risk
Very-
High

Escape

Yes

No

Risk
Extreme

Danger Level	Action
Moderate	Modify
High	Abandon
Very High	Terminate
Extreme	Escape

Return to Problem
Definition

No

Figure 11. Operational Decision Making (ODM)

Discussion of ODM

The following provides some additional discussion concerning the operational decision algorithm on the previous page.

Moderate-risk conditions: This is where the situation reflects a rising risk profile with respect to the operation. Risk could emanate from any number of sources, and thus the operation will be impacted. For moderate-risk conditions, a modification to the operation or mission plan is necessary to prevent the risk from becoming excessive.

High-risk conditions: This is where an encountered event has brought into the operation a dangerous situation. The danger may be not only to the operation but to the organization as well. In this case, the current operation must be abandoned and an alternate operation implemented. Some delay in alternative plan implementation is acceptable. The alternative plan should have already been developed. Most operations fail because of the unrealistic belief that an alternate course of action will not be necessary.

Very high-risk conditions: The danger level in this case has been increasing and continues to do so. The encountered event represents unexpected danger, and thus decisive action is essential. Therefore, to prevent catastrophe, the operation or mission must be terminated. *This must be done without delay.*

Extreme risk conditions: Extreme danger, most likely brought about by a number of unexpected events, relates to impending catastrophe. In this case, the operation must immediately cease and an escape executed. In the ocean, this would almost certainly involve deploying the lifeboats. In aviation, this is well understood as requiring the execution of a specified escape maneuver.

Part IV
Critical Thinking Template

Critical Thinking Template
Orientation

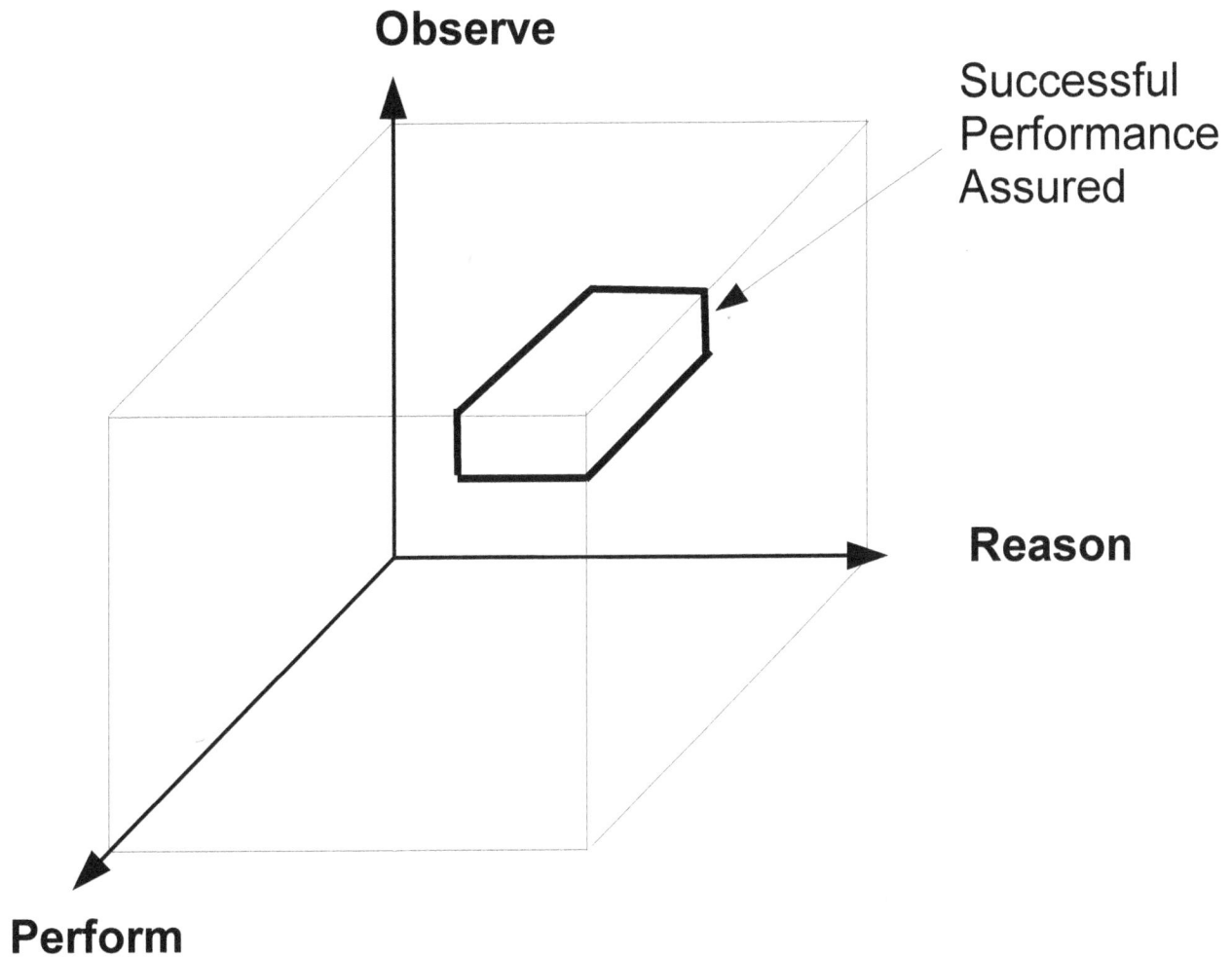

Figure 12. Helpful Orientation for the Critical Thinking Template

Critical Thinking Model Mobile App Depiction

	Clarify	Reason	Win
	Clarify the Actual	Employ Analytic Reasoning	Perform with Precision and Win
Observe with Accuracy and Clarify the Actual — **Situate**	XX		
Detect	XX		
Orient	XX		
Employ Analytic Reasoning — **Analyze**		XX	
Evaluate		XX	
Decide		XX	
Perform with Precision and Win — **Execute**			XX
Measure			XX
Optimize			XX

Table 4. Critical Thinking Model Mobile App Depiction

Clarify the actual, employ reason, perform with precision—win!

Critical Thinking Template

What follows is a discussion of the critical thinking template. In more modern terms, we can think of such a template as an app. The home page of such an app is shown above. This representation contains the motto and a more detailed description of the critical thinking three-step process along the top. Along the left side, the breakout of the three-step process into the nine subgroups is presented.

The idea is to select one of the nine subgroups in descending order as one goes about employing the critical thinking model.

When a subgroup is selected, a corresponding page will be displayed. All such pages are presented in this section. For example, when the critical thinking category "Orient" is selected on the app, the corresponding page is displayed such that this aspect of critical thinking is fully explained.

OBSERVE

Situate   Detect   Orient

Situate: Situate yourself to be able to detect incoming information.

- Find a favorable position or location.

- Activate all sensors, including intuition.

- Establish proper mind-set.

Comment: Often our mind-set is such that important signals are not understood, or worse, may not have been detected.

Caution: Activate radar. Do not fall asleep at the switch, and do not allow your consciousness to turn in on itself.

OBSERVE

Situate **Detect** Orient

Detect: Detect incoming signals and determine what needs attention.

- Focus on signals that may prove significant.

- Locate source of signal (very important).

- Select out signals that rise to event status for further analysis.

- Reorient focus from data to events.

Comment: Avoid those signals that are distracting. An event is something that needs the operator's or manager's attention. Think in terms of *events*, not discrete data items.

OBSERVE

Situate   Detect   **Orient**

Orient: Orient the event or event set in order to clarify the actual. Use clarification tools to help.

- Orient the event on the risk continuum to determine its risk-producing properties.

- Orient the event within the operational environment in which it legitimately resides.

- Orient the event set on the event horizon to further clarify the actual.

Problem Definition
&
Challenge Statement

Problem Definition: What is the problem for which you are seeking a solution? (Avoid any reference to a possible solution.)

_____

_____

_____

Challenge Statement: What challenges will be faced on the journey to find and implement a solution? It is important to acknowledge systems' laws, operational constraints, and best practices.

_____

_____

_____

Remember complex systems behave counter-intuitively:
That is the plausible tends to be wrong.

—J. W. Forrester

REASON

Analyze Evaluate Decide

Analyze: Utilize *analytic reasoning* whenever the situation warrants it. Use empirical reasoning for less important matters.

- Generate solution options, often called alternatives, using an alternative generator designed for this purpose.[1]

- Look for creative solutions to the stated problem and challenge.

- List all candidate alternatives.

A

B

C

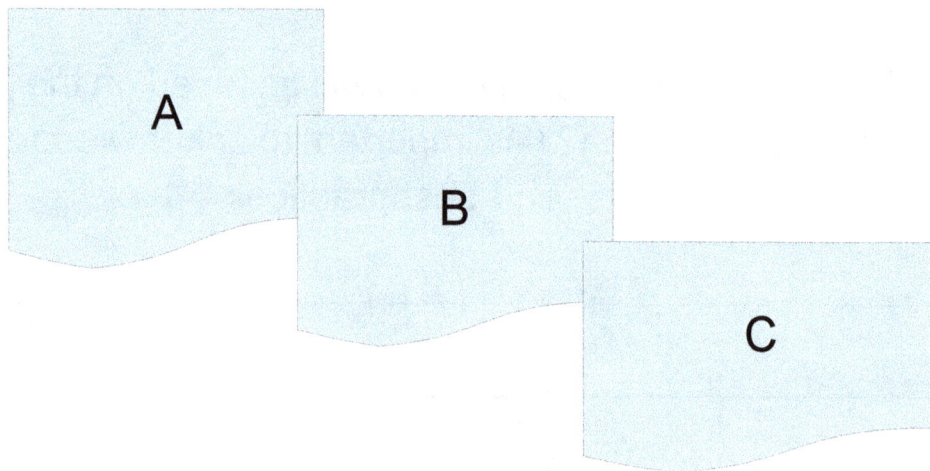

Figure 13. Analysis of A, B, C

---

1   A particularly useful alternative generator is presented on page 30.

REASON

Analyze **Evaluate** Decide

Evaluate: Evaluate each alternative against a set of criteria based on the concept of how effective it will likely be in addressing the problem.

- Determine the intrinsic value of each alternative.

- Determine the probability that this alternative can be applied to the aforementioned problem.

- Multiply each value times the probability.

- Specify the utility of each.

- Utility = Value × Probability

REASON

Analyze   Evaluate   **Decide**

Decide: Decide the best course of action given that you have clearly understood the problem.

- Select the best option (alternative) from a list of possible options. Maximize utility.

- Consider nontraditional solutions.

- Subject each alternative to a test of reasonableness.

Comment: The reasonable man theory is a good way to think about your selection.

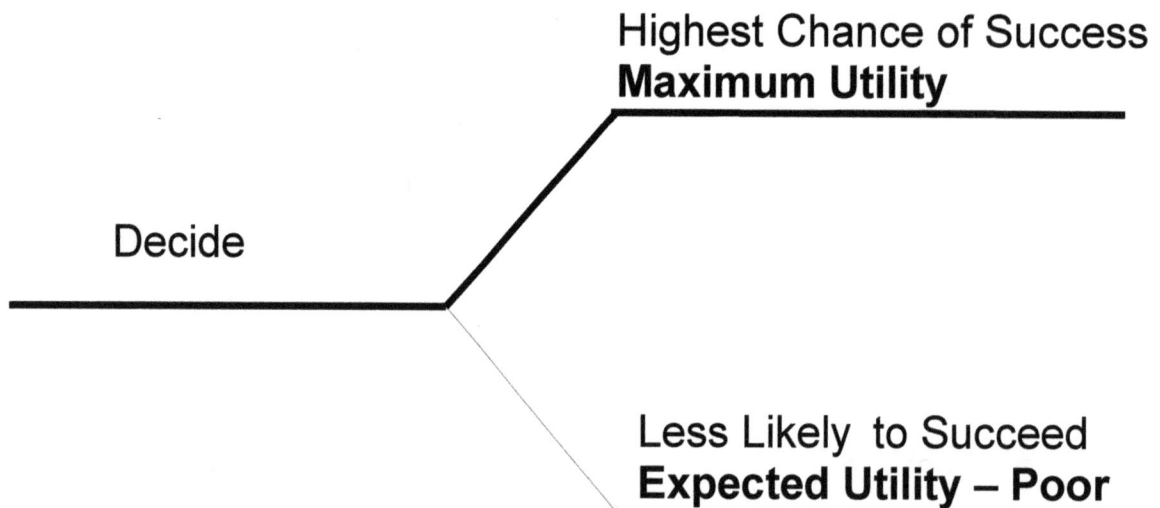

Highest Chance of Success
Maximum Utility

Decide

Less Likely to Succeed
Expected Utility – Poor

Figure 14. Maximum Utility

PERFORM

Execute   Measure   Optimize

Execute: Execute the best option (alternative). This is your choice because it will most effectively deal with the problem at hand.

- In selecting the best alternative, make sure that this option is clearly understood by all players.

- Be prepared to be wrong.

- Stay objective.

- Specify the needed steps in a particular performance package.

- Provide this performance package to all players.

Decisive action is often necessary, so execution should not be unnecessarily delayed. Do not allow the problem to fester.

PERFORM

Execute **Measure** Optimize

Measure: Install performance measures to determine "how goes it."

- Measure performance that will bring credit on your professional skills.

- Make sure that performance measures are meaningful.

- Disregard vanity measures.

Comment: Performance measures are often neglected, especially in large, complex programs of government-run initiatives. It is almost as if many of us do not like bad news.

PERFORM

Execute   Measure   **Optimize**

Optimize: Optimize performance of the ongoing operation by applying timely corrective action to any deviations or deficiencies.

- Make sure that resource management is being appropriately applied.

- Clearly identify when the operation has gone off track.

- Quickly recover from all off track conditions.

Comment: Detect deviations early and make small corrections as in figure 15. Do not wait until deviations become large.

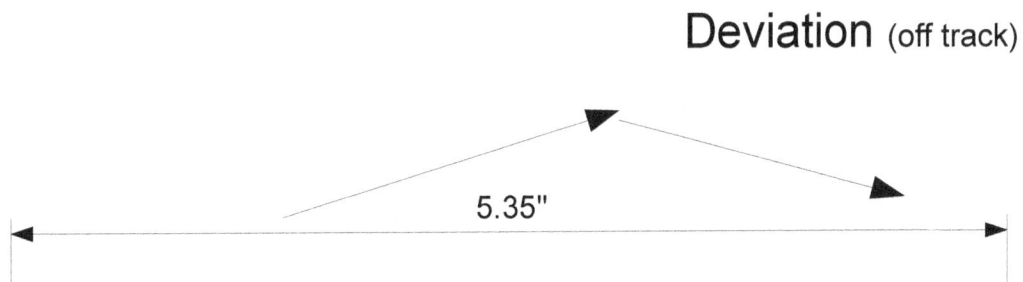

Deviation (off track)

5.35"

Figure 15. Deviation

PERFORM

Execute   Measure   **Optimize**

Represented here is a useful performance tool to assist in optimizing performance. This tool is most useful in dealing with difficult or critical problems associated with large-scale systems. It also assumes that an action plan has been developed and implemented. It is based on a symmetrical matrix depicting "actual" versus "should." As the plan progresses and activities are preformed, certain situations or events will likely be encountered. These events may prove to be mission critical and thus a reevaluation of the mission plan will be necessary. The level of criticality should necessarily encourage the type of action needed.

Should \ Actual	Continue	Modify	Abandon	Terminate	Escape
Continue					
Modify					
Abandon					
Terminate					
Escape					

Table 5. Optimizing Risk Management and Catastrophe Prediction

Also notice that the arrow or trajectory with respect to the appropriate response package depicts whether the situation is on track, leading to success, or off track, leading to failure.

Execute   Measure   **Optimize**

A useful performance management tool is presented here. This tool uses a matrix format with weekly segments along the top and work packages arranged to be completed each week. You can see that for a project or operation to remain on track, package A, for example, must be completed during week 1, and so forth, for the other packages.

Week / Activity	Week 1	Week 2	Week 3	Week 4
Work Package A				
Work Package B				
Work Package C				
Work Package D				

Table 6. Optimize Workflow in Project Activities

Part V

Summary

Critical Thinking Model

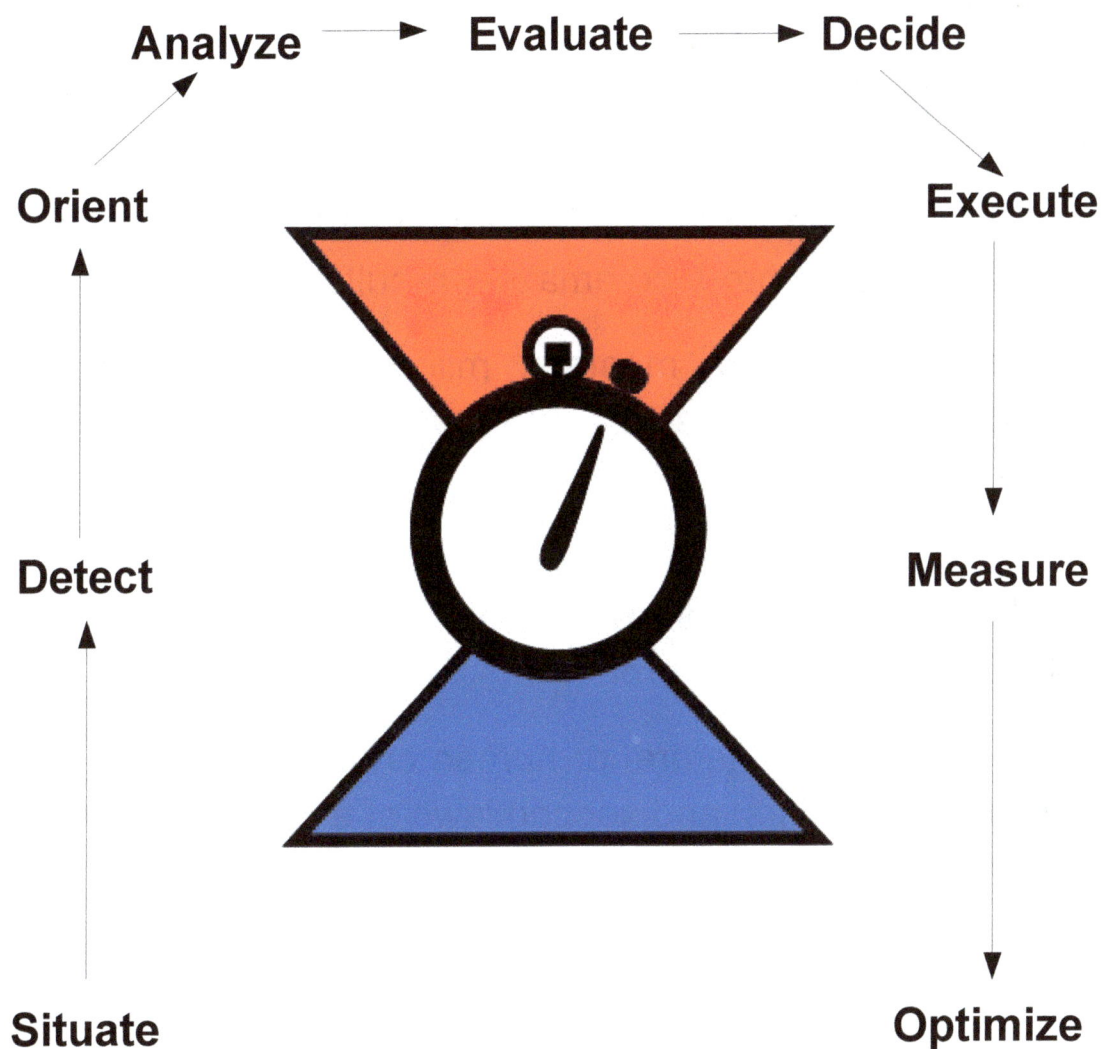

Figure 16. Critical Thinking Model

Helpful Hints

- Critical thinking: An idea whose time has come. This is because as individuals and as a nation we must improve our problem-solving abilities.

- Critical thinking motto: Clarify-Reason-Win. Clarify the actual. Employ reason. Gain winning performance.

- In life, what is most important is not *what* you think but *how* you think. Critical thinking is key.

- Our most important decision: Either we *embrace reason* or do that which is *hostile to reason*.

- Critical thinking can be learned, lends itself to practice, and when used with intent will produce amazing results.

- Airline captains, chess masters, military commanders, military pilots, Top Gun instructors, top managers—all attest to the power of critical thinking.

- When dealing with complexity, such as large-scale systems, remember that these systems will behave counterintuitively: that is, the plausible tends to be wrong.

- All systems, whether natural or human created, must be designed consistent with the first and second laws of energy. Otherwise, they will not work because they cannot work.

- The single greatest cause of catastrophic events such as airline disasters, battlefield losses, business failures, etc., is the well-intentioned but disastrous attempt to apply the *right* solution to the *wrong* problem.

Part VI

Commitment to Reason

Book Series

About the Series

The Commitment to Reason book series is about critical thinking, or more specifically, about applied critical thinking. This initiative includes books, handbooks, podcasts, instructional videos, and newsletters. All of this is intended to make critical thinking more accessible to more people.

Commitment to Reason is based on the premise that what is important is not *what* you think but *how* you think. How to think well then is our goal. This is where critical thinking essentials come to the rescue.

First and foremost, critical thinking encourages us to face a fundamental choice: either we *embrace reason* or do that which is *hostile to reason*.

In this series, we explore not only how to embrace reason in all of its useful formulations but also what we have done (as a nation) that is indeed hostile to reason. The equation is simple. If it is hostile to reason, it will not work because it cannot work.

We look at certain things that are hostile to reason so as to bring some urgency to the issue of whether we need to individually, and collectively as a society, improve our critical thinking skills.

Commitment to Reason
Book Series

Book I: *Hostile to Reason* I. This book introduces the reader to critical thinking and, using some of its principles, critically examines certain aspects of our culture that are based on ideas and concepts that are hostile to reason. A number of new ideas are presented.

Book II: *Hostile to Reason* II. This book covers additional material on critical thinking and continues the theme that certain aspects of our culture are based on that which is hostile to reason. Together books I and II outline the urgent need to improve our judgment and problem-solving abilities.

Book III: *Commit to Reason* I. This book is a practical application of critical thinking essentials for everyday applications. It puts forth the proposition that critical thinking is accessible to almost everyone, is a skill that can be taught, lends itself to practice, and when used with intent will produce amazing results. A companion handbook is also available (see below).

Book IV: *Commit to Reason* II. This book presents a more in-depth discussion of critical thinking essentials and is most useful to professionals in high-stress occupations. Important nonlinear problem-solving strategies are covered, along with a number of real-world examples.

Additional Materials

Books

- *Thinking, Fast and Slow* by Daniel Kahneman. Presents a detailed explanation of various forms of reasoning errors. Author was the winner of the Nobel Prize in economics.
- *Think Like a Freak* by Stephan Levitt and Stephan Dubner. An enjoyable journey into the world of mental confusion and mistakes.
- *Decisive* by the Heath Brothers. An analysis of good and bad decisions.
- *Hostile to Reason*, books I and II, by Captain Kevin M. Smith. Provides a crash course on critical thinking and then examines certain aspects of our culture that are based on ideas that are hostile to reason.

Instructional Videos by The Great Courses

- *The Philosopher's Toolkit* by Patrick Grimm. A good introduction to critical thinking.
- *The Creative Thinker's Toolkit* by Gerard Puccio. Additional material on critical thinking.
- *Your Deceptive Mind* by Stephan Novella. A good description of thinking errors and some ways to improve our ability to reason.
- *The Art and Science of Critical Decision Making* by Roberto. A good discussion of decision making from a manager's perspective.
- *Argumentation* by David Zarefsky. How to create a winning argument.

Other Instructional Videos

- *Intelligent Systems and the Age of the Superfunction* by Captain Kevin M. Smith. EISBN 97 81 46 66 96 945. Produced by MKP Technologies, September 2015. Applies critical thinking to one of the most pressing challenges of the day - management of complexity.

Captain Kevin M. Smith
USN (Ret.)

Aviator, Author, Speaker

precisionaviator@gmail.com

*Figure 17. The Supersonic F-8 Crusader
flown by Captain Kevin M. Smith*